Prep:
Paint the edge of all heart pages Pink. Let dry.
Apply *Stickles* glitter glue. Let dry. Turn pieces
over. Paint and glitter as on the front side.

Cover:
Adhere decorative papers, chipboard diecuts
and buttons with ribbons.

For all pages:
Adhere decorative papers, diecuts, stickers,
ribbons, rhinestones and buttons tied with ribbons. Add extra sparkle by touching diecuts,
chipboard and papers with glitter glue.

Button Frame:
Cut a paper 4" diameter circle. Adhere to page.
Tie ribbons through colored buttons and
adhere around the circle perimeter. For a more
dimensional look, overlap the edges of some of
the buttons.

Tags:
Increase your journaling and photo space by
adding tags between the pages. Paint the edges
of the tags in the same manner as the pages.
Adhere decorative papers, chipboard, stickers,
rhinestones, ribbons and buttons as desired.

Tip:

For more color and dimension, tie ribbon
to the binder ring and between each of
the pages and tags.

Terina Matthews

*Terina has been
a designer and scrap-
book teacher for 12
years. She has been
scrapbooking since
she was 10 years
old. Her favorite
scrapbooks track the
lives of her children as they grow.*

Sunny Florida

by Nicole Patrizio

Vacations are a time for taking photos and collecting memories of wonderful experiences. Showcase your love for sunny places with these great techniques.

SIZE: 8" diameter

MATERIALS:

Clear Scraps Flower album • Decorative paper • Chipboard • Ribbon • Rub-ons • Epoxy stickers • Buttons • Pebbles Pom-Poms • Pebbles Applicator • Eyelets • Metal embellishments • *Ranger* Star Dust Stickles • Acrylic paint • Foam brush • Mod Podge • *We R Memory Keepers* Crop-A-Dile • Sewing machine • Stapler • Adhesives

1. Paint the shaped edge of the acrylic and the chipboard petals.

2. Punch a hole in the page and petal with a Crop-A-Dile.

3. Secure petal to page with an eyelet.

4. Adhere buttons on the back side of the eyelets.

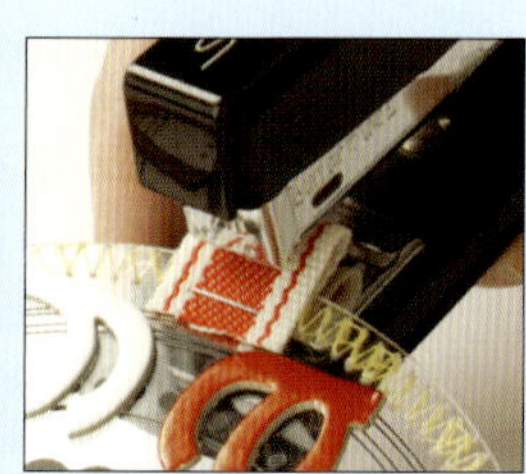

5. Staple folded ribbon to the edge to form a tab.

Nicole Patrizio
While much of Nicole's scrapping revolves around her family and anything she finds inspiring, her deepest scrapping passion finds expression in her vacation albums.

Tip:

Rub-on words are easy to apply to photos. Simply choose a position that enhances the photo. "Hot Sun" and "Serenity" are excellent examples of great positioning.

Avoid overpowering your photos with embellishments. Often, less is more. Small accents like the tiny sun sticker add dimension without being distracting. Notice the tiny glittering butterfly and the penstitched flight trail - a charming and simple addition.

The lace diecut creates the illusion that you are looking out from a window while the scroll captures the movement of the reeds.

Sunny Florida - Prep for all pages:
Paint the shaped edge of the acrylic and the chipboard petals. Let dry. Seal all painted edges with Mod Podge. Punch holes in the acrylic edge and attach chipboard petals with eyelets. On the back of the page, cover the eyelet with a button.
• Cut photos into circles that fit the page and adhere in place. Fold a ribbon and staple to the edge to make a tab.

Sunny Florida - Front Cover:
Zigzag stitch around the edge with a sewing machine. Apply rub-ons. Adhere chipboard letters. Staple ribbon tab in place.

Sunny Florida - Back of Front Cover:
Adhere double-sided decorative paper over the center rub-on.

XOXO:
Notice how the etching shows through the cover beautifully. This effect works best with letters that look the same from both front and back.

I Love You:
Adhere decorative paper, photo, clear tag, ribbons, and stickers. Decorate the clear tag with a White Souffle pen and a Red heart sticker.

Flowers and Buttons:
Adhere flower, photo and decorative paper to hide the adhesive from the front of the page. Add buttons and stickers.

Fun Frame:
Cut a frame from decorative paper and adhere to page so the photo on the next page will show. Adhere decorative paper, shaped acrylic arrow, buttons and stickers to page.

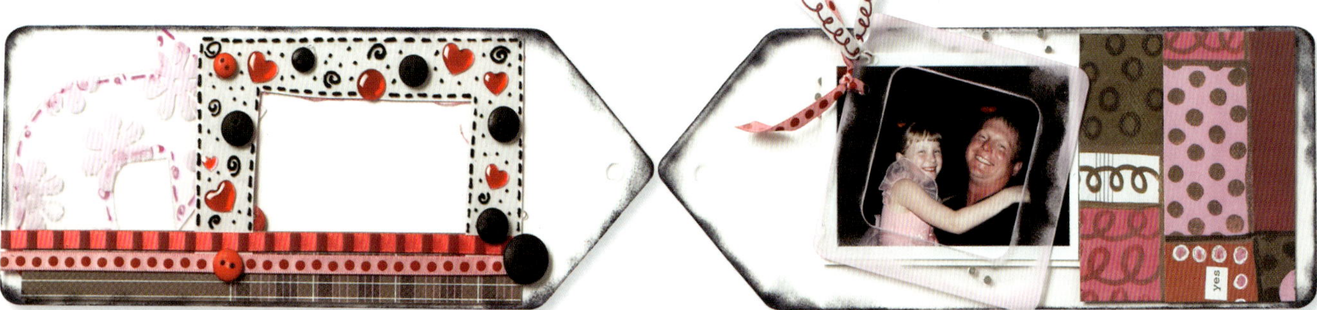

Framing Technique:
Hide the adhesive from the front of the page with ribbons, stickers and buttons.

So Happy Together:
Adhere photo so it will show through the frame on the previous page. Adhere decorative papers. Daub StazOn Opaque Pink ink around the edges of the frame. Punch 2 holes in the frame. Tie ribbons through holes. Adhere frame over photo.

Love, Love, Love:
Adhere decorative papers and photo to hide the adhesive from the front of the page. Add rhinestones.

Back Cover:
Daub circles onto page with Black StazOn ink.

Hugs and Kisses Tag Album

by Janet Blair

Fill a clear tag album with hugs, kisses, photos and many loving memories.

SIZE: 4" x 10"

MATERIALS:

Clear Scraps (Angled Tag album, Arrow shapes, Slide) • Decorative paper • Fabric paper • Stickers • Ribbon • Buttons
• Flower stamp • *Tsukineko* StazOn inkpads (Black, Blush Pink) • Dauber • *Sakura* pens (White Souffle, Pink gel, Black glaze)
• *EK Success* Inscriblio Engraving tool • Adhesive

Cover:
Print "XOXO" on paper. Lay cover over printed letters. Etch the letters into the cover. Add penstitching around the letters with a White Souffle pen. Add squiggles and dots around the edge of the cover.

Prep:
Ink the edges of each page with Black StazOn.

1. Lay cover over printed letters. Etch the cover using the etching tool.

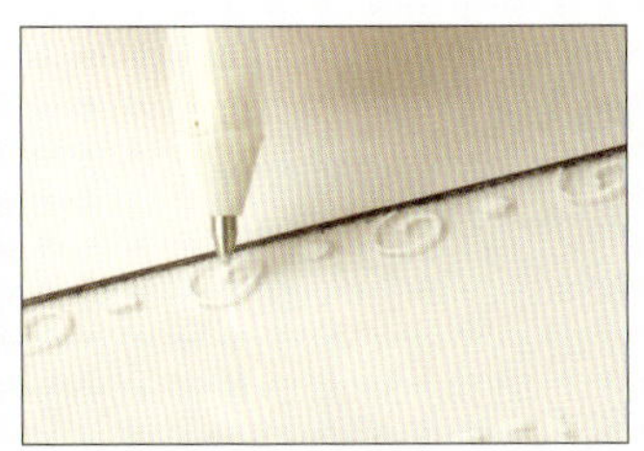

2. Add penstitching around the letters and squiggles around the edge.

3. Doodle I, heart, U and make dots around the edge of the straight arrow.

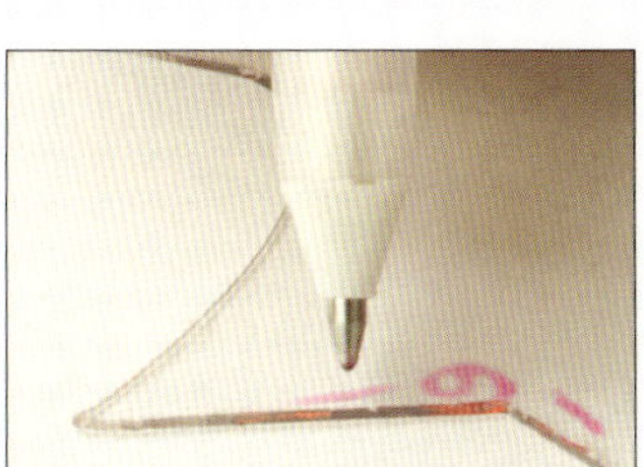

4. Draw dashes and squiggles on the edge of the front side of the curved arrow.

5. Stamp the back side of the curved arrow with StazOn ink.

6. Daub StazOn Opaque Pink ink around the edges of the frame.

7. Daub circles onto page with Black StazOn ink.

Tip: Adhere a matted journaling circle to hide the adhesive on the front cover.

Add variety and interest to your album by covering some pages entirely with decorative papers, photo, journaling circle, letter stickers, flowers held together with brads, ribbons, and rhinestones.

Alcohol inks can be used to tint acrylic pages. Simply mask off the area you are not coloring and tint desired areas before embellishing. Also, don't neglect your stamp collection. Create fabulous texture and beautiful design using rubber stamps and StazOn ink. Mount swirl stamp on clear acrylic block. Tap the stamp on top of the Timber Brown ink pad and carefully place it on the acrylic without sliding the stamp. Repeat until the entire panel is covered with swirls.

Create your own round journaling blocks using a paper cup, pencil, scissors, and lined cardstock. Simply trace around the cup, cut out the circle, cut a circular mat and adhere to page. The page looks better from both sides if you place journaling blocks on both sides, or use a double-sided decorative paper for the mat.
Tip: If using a solid color mat, stamp a pretty design on the back of the page over the mat in a contrasting color. This project uses a stamped Butterfly in White StazOn ink on the back cover.

Lisa Falduto

A freelance paper craft designer, Lisa has been published numerous times in magazines and idea books. She loves to travel and teach classes to paper crafting enthusiasts everywhere!

Crayon Album

by Lisa Falduto

The Story of a Budding Little Artist is told with creative flair in this crayon-shaped album dedicated to a child's artful endeavors. This album is the perfect shape for collecting these special memories. Record your unique story on circular journaling spaces for a very personal preservation of a special journey.

SIZE: 4" x 11"

MATERIALS:
Clear Scraps (Crayon album) • Decorative papers • Rub-ons • Butterfly transparency • Rhinestones • Ribbon • *Autumn Leaves* Swirl stamp • Clear acrylic block • *Tsukineko* StazOn Timber Brown inkpad • *Ranger* (Cut n Dry foam; Alcohol inks: Butterscotch, Lettuce) • Paper cup • Adhesive

1. Daub alcohol ink onto the flower shape.

2. Stamp an image onto the pages with StazOn ink.

Prep:
Stamp the swirl onto the front and back covers and page 4 with StazOn ink. Cut 5 circles from decorative papers for journaling. Adhere a strip of decorative paper along the short edge of each page.

Cover:
Color the tip of the crayon with alcohol inks. Cut cardstock to fit the center of the acrylic flower. Attach flowers to the center and write the title around the edge of the circle. Daub alcohol ink onto the acrylic flower. Adhere acrylic flower with mat to the cover. Adhere a strip of decorative paper along the outer edge.

Baby - A page

Design possibilities open when you choose rub-ons that look beautiful from both sides. Apply rub-ons to page. Add brads to flower centers. Adhere diecut word and flowers.

Baby - Back of A page

Clip a calendar for journaling to the page. Adhere rhinestone flower.

Baby - B page

Rub-ons take on real zing when you apply rhinestones in place of the flowers. Adhere rhinestones and diecut word to page.

Baby - Back of B page

Tip: For a pleasing look on both sides of the album, hide the adhesive by duplicating accents. Note the rhinestone flowers are in the same position on both sides of the page.

Baby - Y page

Using similar accents throughout gives your album a unified look. Remember, accents should complement rather than overwhelm your photo.

Baby - Back Cover

The entire back page has been left for journaling... on a circle diecut and decorative paper for recording thoughts.

Baby Book

by Laura McCollough
Nothing is as precious as a child. This shaped album is a charming way to share the moments as your little one grows.

SIZE: 5" x 11"

MATERIALS:
Clear Scraps (Baby album, Clear tag) • Decorative paper • Mini brads • Metal clips • Chipboard letters • Glitter diecuts • Rub-ons • Rhinestones • Rhinestone flowers • Flowers • Ribbon • Rick-rack • Pen • Adhesive

Baby - Front cover

Prep: Adhere papers with mounted photos to the back of each page so it shows through the front.

A word about Adhesives: Use adhesive in small amounts and in places that will be covered up.

Tip: Cut rhinestone flourishes to the desired sizes and place them on the front sides of the acrylic letters. Adhere diecuts, and other embellishments to the front of the pages.

Baby - Inside Front Cover - B page
Embellish this page with decorative paper, rick-rack and accessories.

Baby - Inside Front Cover
Adhere glitter letters, diecuts, and rick-rack to page.

Tips:

Add journaling wherever you can. The entire back page is for recording precious memories, You can journal on tags, diecuts, or papers. Attach them to the pages with clips.

Laura McCollough
This California scrapper has enjoyed scrapbooking all her life and is passionate about sharing this art form with others.
Check out her blog at:
http:akissonthechic.typepad.com.

PHOTOS & PAGES:
See page 12.

SIZE: 6" x 8"

MATERIALS:
• *Clear Scraps* Crown album
• *Cuttlebug* (Embossing machine, Swirls embossing folder)
• *Sakura* pens (White Souffle, Pink gel)
• Pastel rhinestones
• Rhinestone frames
• Rub-ons
• Stickers
• Ribbons
• Silk flowers
• Diecut flowers
• Adhesive

Front Cover:
Dot the edge with a Souffle pen. Adhere photo and rhinestones. Emboss a clear tag and color with a Pink gel pen. Attach the tag and ribbons to the binder rings.

Inside Back Cover: Capture a Moment
Adhere photo, diecut flower and rhinestone stickers.

Diamond Crown:
Apply diamond shaped rub-ons.

1. Purchase blank albums.

2. Use a Souffle pen to dot around the edge.

3. Adhere rhinestones.

4. Apply rub-ons to background.

"Clearly a Princess" Album

by Janet Blair

Shaped albums are a lot of fun, especially when the shape reflects the theme as in this Princess album. Adding rhinestones gives the extra sparkle that we all love.

ADDITIONAL PHOTOS & PAGES: See page 11.

Flower pages:
Adhere large flower to hide the adhesive for the photo. Adhere a sticker over the flower center.

Princess:
Draw spirals at random on the page with a White Souffle pen. Adhere photo, stickers and rub-ons.

Smile! page 4:
Draw dashes with White Souffle pen around the edge of the page. Add rhinestones and rub-ons.

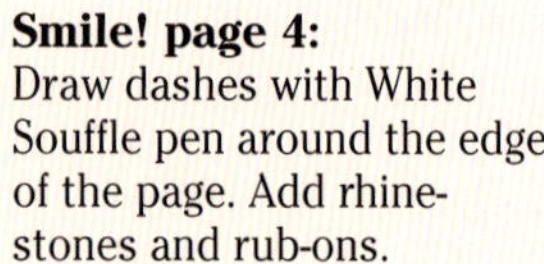

All Dressed Up - page 6:
Draw dashes with Pink Souffle pen around the edge of the page. Add photo, ribbon, rhinestones, and stickers.

1. Mask the top and bottom of the tree. Rub the star onto the Mustard StazOn inkpad.

2. Rub the base onto the Brown StazOn inkpad.

3. Swipe the Forest Green inkpad over the tree.

Tips:

This album is constructed from the back page, layering up. The last page is the full tree with the star.

Julie Howard

"Scrapbooking makes me feel like an artist", shared Julie. She loves being creative and preserving family memories at the same time.

SIZE: 7½" x 11"

MATERIALS:
Clear Scraps (Christmas Tree album) • Decorative paper • *Tsukineko* StazOn inkpads (Forest Green, Mustard Yellow, Timber Brown) • Punches (Balloon, Circle) • Metal star • Stickers • Ribbons • Wire • Miniature Christmas tree light garland • Adhesive

For pages with star and trunk:
Mask the star top and bottom trunk of the tree.
Swipe the Forest Green StazOn inkpad across the tree section. Let dry.
Remove the mask.
Rub the star onto the Mustard StazOn inkpad. Rub the trunk on the Timber Brown inkpad. Let dry.

All other pages:
Swipe the Forest Green inkpad over the page. Let dry.
Cut photo circles to fit the ornament circles. Adhere to tree.
Add stickers.
Wrap page with tree light ornaments.
Adhere bear sticker to the bottom of the page.
Adhere decorative paper to the back of the sticker.

Tree Album
by Julie Howard

Christmas albums are always a favorite. Spice up yours with a unique shape and dimensional decorations for a delightful record of those wonderful wintry family gatherings.

Class at the Farm - inside of back cover

Emboss an acrylic heart shape with the Cuttlebug and ink with StazOn "Blazing Red." Immediately wipe off the ink for a lighter look. The corrugated letters were cut from Starbuck's coffee cozies.

Farm Buildings - side pages

Cover the page with Red cardstock, add a photo and photo corner made from corrugated cardstock. Punch holes for threading the twine with a Crop-A-Dile. The flower centers are circles cut from corrugated paper and tied in the center with twine. Adhere flowers to page.

Sunflower center page -

Add texture to the flower centers by embossing them with a Cuttlebug machine. The watering can is a clear embellishment that has been embossed, inked, and decorated with Silver duct tape on the spout, top and bottom.

Side pages -

Adhere photos, decorative papers and clip-art to cover up the items that show through from the other side. Notice the tractor overlaying the heart; this is a nice way to hide the adhesive.

AnnCaryl Worland

AnnCaryl is a retired art teacher who has been crafting since she was a child. An experienced paper artist, she appreciates the exciting possibilities of clear acrylic as a medium. She loves to scrapbook as well as make cards and minibooks.

Tip:

The White accent dots on all of the Clear Scrap flower shapes were added using the Souffle pen by Sakura.

Barn - inside of back cover:

Print tiny photos on adhesive paper. Cut out photos and place as shingles on the roof. Diecut the pig from a scrap of acrylic sheet and texture with the Cuttlebug. Dry brush with acrylic paint. Adhere to page.

Side flaps:

Adhere photos back to back to hide the adhesive. The sunflower cardstock from the front looks great from the back as well.

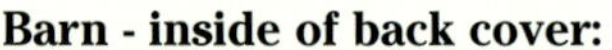

by AnnCaryl Worland
Our class visited the Weston Red Barn Farm! Field trips are always enjoyable. If you go, take lots of photos and preserve the experience in a wonderful album.

SIZE: 8" x 9½"

MATERIALS:
Clear Scraps (School House album, flowers, hearts, arrows, 6"x 6" sheet)
• Cardstock • Decorative paper
• Corrugated craft paper • Diecut tag
• Screw brads • Jute • Flowers
• Ribbons • *Prostripe* automotive ¼" pin stripe tape • Acrylic paint • Black permanent pen • Brown marker • Chalk
• *Sakura* White Souffle pen • *Autumn Leaves* Clear flower stamp • *Tsukineko* StazOn inkpad (Blazing Red, Timber Brown) • *We R Memory Keepers* Crop-A-Dile • *Sizzix* diecut pig • *Provo Craft* (Cricut machine, Sunflower die)
• *Cuttlebug* (Embossing machine, embossing folders: stylized flowers, heart blocks, bloom dots) • Punches (⅛" circle, photo corner) • Silver duct tape
• Adhesive

Barn - Front cover

Adhere photos. Use automotive stripe tape to make the door trim. Punch small holes in the outer edge with the Crop-a-Dile and stitch with jute. Tie knots at each end to secure. To make the closure, punch a hole with the Crop-a-Dile and insert screw brads. Tie twine to one brad and wrap in a figure eight to close the album.

1. Punch holes with a Crop-A-Dile and weave jute through the holes.

2. Ink all album edges with Red StazOn ink.

3. Apply pinstripe tape to make the barn doors.

4. Use a White Souffle pen to make dots around the edge.

5. Adhere flowers to the page.

Barn - Back cover

Adhere cardstock to make a barn. Trim corrugated paper to fit the opening in the window and adhere to form a frame. Cut photos in circles and adhere. Journal around each photo. Adhere a diecut sunflower. Trim decorative paper to look like a nest and adhere to the bottom of both sides of the window sill. Cut out 2 roosters, 1 a mirror image. Adhere them together back to back and place in the window so they can be seen from both sides.

Holly Album

by Julie Howard

Pets enhance our quality of life and help us live longer. Every pet owner has a collection of photos of Fluff or Spot. This album is a tribute to Holly, the family dog. Make a special album for your favorite four-legged friend today.

SIZE: 5" x 10"

MATERIALS:

Clear Scraps (Dog bone album, frame, tag) • *Cuttlebug* (Embossing machine, Embossing folders: stylized flowers, tiny mosaic texture, small stars) • Acrylic paint (Brown, White, Green, Yellow) • Chipboard (letters, heart) • Metal buckle • Stickers • Flowers • Minibrads • Leather half circle • Decorative papers • Ribbons • Twill • Cardstock • Pawprint stamp • *Tsukineko* StazOn Black ink • *Ranger* alcohol inks (Latte, Ginger) • Jump rings • Metal charms • Red metal clips • Pink heart clip • *Sakura* Souffle pen • Good Dog metal plate • *Bind It All* O-wire • *We R Memory Keepers* Crop-A-Dile • *Provo Craft* (Cricut machine, Paper pups cartridge) • Paper towel • Adhesive

Holly - Front Cover

Emboss cover using the Cuttlebug and tiny mosaic folder. With the bumpy side face down, paint the cover and wipe away leaving the paint in the raised squares only. Paint chipboard letters. Let dry. Tie ribbon around the "y" and through the hole in the edge of the metal heart. Adhere letters to cover. Wrap ribbon around the cover and secure to buckle with a brad. Adhere ribbon, metal hearts, and leather semi-circle in place. Write the title on the leather piece.

Holly - Back Cover

Adhere papers to cover adhesives from the other side. Try not to cover too much of the star. Attach tags to diecut bones with eyelets. Tie string through eyelets and adhere to page. Emboss and paint a scrap of clear acrylic as for the cover. Cut into a tag shape. Adhere photo to tag. Adhere to page.

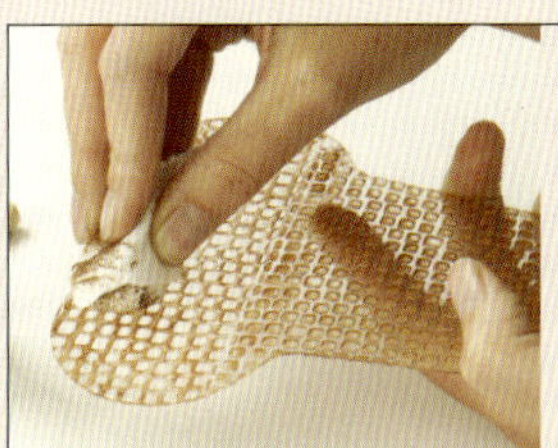

1. Paint embossed cover and wipe away with a paper towel.

2. Paint the edges of pages with Brown acrylic ink.

3. Drip alcohol inks onto frame.

4. Punch holes in the bottom of the page with a Crop-A-Dile.

5. Attach flowers with brads

6. Attach White tag to page with binder wire. Tie ribbons around wire before closing.

Holly - back of cover
Attach flowers to photo with Mini brads. Adhere photo, chipboard pieces and layered papers. Tie Black thread around the chipboard bone, adhere to round tag and glue to page.

Holly - page 1
Emboss one end of the page using the Cuttlebug and stylized daisy folder. Paint the stems and flowers from the back side with acrylic paint. Paint edges Brown. Let dry. Adhere cardstock and photo to hide the adhesive on the other side. Adhere chipboard letter.

Holly - page 2
Adhere papers, photo, and chipboard letter to page.

Holly - page 3
Stamp one end of page with paw prints and star. Adhere matted photo and letter. Punch holes in the bottom of the page and attach dangling charms with jump rings. Adhere round tag.

Holly - page 4
Tint the clear frame with alcohol inks. Attach to photo with brads. Adhere photo and letter to page. Emboss and paint a scrap of clear acrylic as for the cover. Diecut a star. Paint the star edge. Punch a hole in the top of the star and tie a ribbon. Adhere to page.

Holly - page 5
Adhere photos, letter, and printed text. Adhere ribbon behind oval metal tag. Adhere metal dog bone to tag. Adhere to page. Adhere clear stickers.

Holly - page 6
Cover one side of page with cardstock for journaling. Adhere tags, clips, and chipboard pieces. Attach brad to the center of the flowers and adhere to page.

Holly - page 7
Adhere vellum "My Dog" and photo to page. Insert brad into flower center and adhere to page. Diecut angel dog and adhere to page. Diecut a scrap of acrylic into a star shape and journal on the star with a Black marker. Adhere to page. Mat metal plate on cardstock. Punch holes in plate and page. Attach to page with binder wire. Tie ribbons around wire.

Silly Girls

by Janet Blair

Celebrate special friendships with an album dedicated to preserving the memories. This 'friends' album provides a fabulous collection of photos of summer camps, dance recitals, school activities and giggles shared with your best friends.

SIZE: 6¾" x 10"

MATERIALS:
Clear Scraps (Arrow album, Half round tag) • Decorative paper • Stickers • Chipboard diecuts • Ribbons • Arrow stamp • *Tsukineko* StazOn Timber Brown inkpad • Dauber • Pink acrylic paint • *Cuttlebug* (Embossing machine, folder) • Sandpaper • Adhesive

Janet Blair

Janet is a very talented graphic designer, scrapbooker and co-owner of Clear Scraps. She searches for new ways to preserve her favorite memories.

Contact her at www.clearscraps.com

Tip:

Adhere double-sided papers, photo, and chipboard to pages so they hide the adhesive on the other side. Add buttons, letter stickers and ribbons as desired. Assemble the album and tie ribbons around the rings. Add a tag embossed with the Cuttlebug machine.

1. Ink the edges of the arrows with Timber Brown StazOn ink.

2. Stamp the back side of an arrow page using Timber Brown StazOn ink.

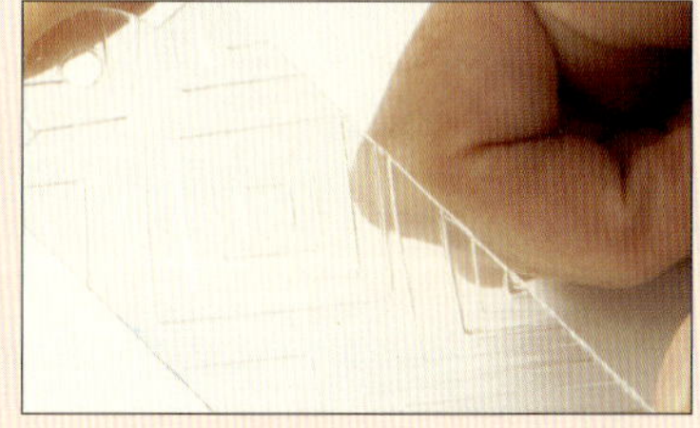

3. Emboss a diecut tag with a Cuttlebug machine.